HARRY TRUMAN

AND THE
LITTLE WHITE HOUSE
IN KEY WEST

In January 1994, David McCullough, Pulitzer Prize winning author of Truman, stands next to the infamous poker table at the Little White House.

HARRY TRUMAN
AND THE
LITTLE WHITE HOUSE
IN KEY WEST

TM

by
Arva Moore Parks

CENTENNIAL PRESS
MIAMI, FLORIDA

Design and Layout First Edition: Cheryl Paige Frary
Third Edition: Scott M. Deems
Cover Design: Scott M. Deems

Third Edition, 2003

©1999 Arva Moore Parks

ISBN 0-9629402-0-8

Published by Centennial Press

1601 South Miami Avenue, Miami, Florida 33129

Printed in United States of America

CONTENTS

KEY WEST, Fla. U.S. N. Wireless Telegraph Station and Commandant's Quarters.

August 28th 1907. Stoped at Key West for five hours.

Quarters A & B as seen in an old Key West postcard.

6

INTRODUCTION

Historians rank Harry S. Truman, 33rd President of the United States, among America's ten best. This is interesting, because he was not particularly popular during his presidency (1945–52). What then are the special qualities of the man and his presidency that have vaulted him into this position in history and have set him apart from other twentieth century presidents?

Harry S. Truman has been called "the last human being" to occupy the White House —"an uncommon, common man." Despite the power and trappings of the office of president of the most powerful nation in the world—a nation fresh from a stunning victory over a host of powerful nations, Harry S. Truman remained more genuinely "home folks" than perhaps any other president in history.

President Truman called the White House the "Great White Jail" and took great pleasure in escaping from it. Next to going home to his beloved Independence, Missouri, his favorite getaway was The Little White House at the Navy Submarine Base in Key West, Florida. From the time of his first visit in November 1946 (just a few days after the Republicans took over Congress for the first time since the distant days of Herbert Hoover) up to and including five post-presidency visits, Key West became the place where, perhaps more than any other, he could unwind, relax and be himself.

But even in this relaxed atmosphere, the business of government was unceasing. "The only thing that would in any way make it look as if it were a vacation," he wrote on November 29, 1951, to his friend Carl Hatch, "is the fact that I do not have the constant stream of visitors all day long and can sit down and get through my document list and catch up with my correspondence. As usual, never a day goes by that I do not have to make some decision which affects the whole of the United States and sometimes the rest of the world. I had one of that sort to make yesterday."

But despite the heavy burden of the presidency, Truman had a way of enjoying himself in Key West. From the journals of the trips, it is possible to document the smallest details of his Key West days. From this, one is struck with the simple fact that even though he worked every day, he, his staff, the press corps and those around him had a lot of fun and struck up a sort of stag party, fraternity house camaraderie when they were there. After each visit, he left smiling and rejuvenated—vowing to return.

7

It was not until after his stunning re-election in 1948 that he was able to convince his wife, Bess, to join him in Key West on his fifth visit. Eventually, Bess and his daughter Margaret shared President Truman's love for Key West and its casual life-style. "We had a good time at Key West on that first visit," (November 1948) Margaret wrote, "everybody was in a mood to clown, do impromptu jigs and laugh their heads off at almost anything."

Truman spent 175 halcyon days in Key West during his presidency. At the restored Key West Little White House, which opened to the public in April 1991, one has the feeling that Truman is still in town and will return momentarily. Perhaps he has gone for a swim at "Truman Beach" or has slipped through the Presidential Gates for a brisk walk through the streets of Key West.

The Key West Little White House Museum gives the American public an unique opportunity to discover a very personal side of Harry Truman and how his down-to-earth-no-nonsense-feet-on-the-ground personality affected his presidency and the events of his day.

QUARTERS A & B

When Quarters A & B were built in 1890, they were on the waterfront.

The original 2.27 acre tract upon which the Little White House is located was purchased by the U.S. Navy in January 1854, at the cost of $10,400.

In 1882, a young civil engineer, Lt. Robert E. Peary, later the famed North Pole explorer, directed the design and construction of a new concrete seawall, which cost $4,000 and ran 572 feet along the water's edge in front of what would be the officers quarters.

Dissatisfaction with the living conditions in Key West rankled naval personnel as early as 1878. One officer wrote there were "no residences belonging to the Navy, and there being no fit boarding houses in the town, married officers are compelled to rent houses and keep up their own establishments."

In 1881, Commandant J.K. Winn continued the complaint that Key West was the only station where no quarters were provided for officers.

Finally, in 1889, the Navy furnished specification for two "Frame Dwellings" to house the base commandant in Quarters "B" and the paymaster in Quarters "A." Architect George McKay detailed two "frame structures, two stories high, without cellars, and surrounded with piazzas both first and second stories."

New York contractor Rowland A. Robbins, with a low bid of $7,489 was awarded the contract on January 15, 1890. Construction began immediately. Commandant Winn's letter of May 17, 1890, reflected on his new personal residence as it neared completion.

"I like the location very much and I believe the houses will be very comfortable. They are certainly very pretty and make an excellent appearance."

Quarters A & B were converted to a single house in the early years of the twentieth century and housed the base commandant.

When the waterfront was filled in and bulkheaded in 1903–1904, Quarters A & B were no longer on the water. In 1942, the Navy built the Administration Building completely blocking the ocean view.

Captain Charles Edwin Reordan (right) commandant of the Key West Submarine Base and wife May (left) pose in the yard with their son, Robert, and their grandaughter, Katy. The Reordans vacated Quarters A & B shortly before it became the Little White House.

During World War I, Thomas Edison took up residence at the Quarters during his six-month stay in Key West while refining his depth charge invention for the Navy.

During World War II, Capt. Charles Edwin Reordan, Commandant of the Naval Operating Base, lived in the house with his wife, May, and his two grandchildren. The Reordans moved from the house in early 1946 when he retired from the Navy. A few months later, President Truman took advantage of the vacant quarters and moved in for the first of his eleven "working vacations."

President Dwight D. Eisenhower met with members of his staff on the Little White House lawn while convalescing from his heart attack in 1956.

The Little White House was reconverted into two houses in June 1953. In 1957, it was again returned to a single family dwelling and designated Quarters A. The furniture and furnishings were returned to their appearance during the Truman era. The Little White House continued to house the base commanders until the naval station closed in 1974.

After Truman's presidency, Presidents Eisenhower and Kennedy also visited the Little White House.

In 1961, President John F. Kennedy met with British Prime Minister Harold MacMillan in Key West during the Bay of Pigs debacle.

Harry S. Truman

THE MAN FROM MISSOURI

"I tried never to forget who I was and where I'd come from and where I was going back to."

Harry S. Truman

Harry S. Truman was born in Lamar, Missouri on May 8, 1884. The "S" in his name was simply an initial. It was used as a compromise between the names of his maternal (Solomon Young) and paternal (Anderson Shipp Truman) grandfathers. The Trumans moved to Independence when Harry was six years old. He graduated from Independence High School in 1901.

The future president of the United States at about six months of age.

Martha Ellen and John Anderson Truman, Harry's parents, on their wedding day, December 28, 1881. John Truman died in 1914, but "Mamma" Truman lived to see her son in the White House.

13

Afflicted with poor eyesight, Harry could not play sports so he took up reading instead. A conscientious student, he once boasted that he had read every book in the Independence Public Library. His love of history and biography had a positive influence on his presidency.

When he graduated from high school, his family could not afford to send him to college and poor eyesight kept him from a West Point appointment. He became a railroad timekeeper and a bank clerk instead. He joined the National Guard in 1905 and a year later returned to the family farm at Grandview. His mother credited his farming days for teaching him his legendary "common sense."

Harry Truman at age 13.

The 1901 Graduating Class of Independence High School poses for posterity. Seventeen year old Harry is fourth from the left in the back row and his future wife, Bess, is on the far right of the second row. Valedictorian Charlie Ross, far left in the first row, would someday become the future president's press secretary.

First Lieutenant Truman of the Missouri National Guard, 1917.

Photograph of Bess that Harry carried to France.

Just a few days after the United States entered World War I, Truman became a lieutenant in the Missouri National Guard. He embarked for France in April 1918 as Captain of Battery "D" 129th Field Artillery. His natural leadership ability earned "Captain Harry" many honors and associations that helped his future political career.

His AEF identity card showed him in a rare pose without his glasses.

"Captain Harry" mounted on horseback in the French village of Coëtquidan.

15

In 1914, Harry bought a second hand Stafford automobile making it easier to get from the Grandview farm to Independence to court Bess.

After a nine year courtship, Harry (35) and Bess (34) were married in Independence on June 28, 1919.

16

Margaret Truman

After the war, Truman married his childhood sweetheart, Elizabeth W. "Bess" Wallace, who he had met in Sunday School when he was six and she was five years old. After their marriage, they moved in with her family at 219 Delaware Street in Independence. It was their home for the rest of their lives. In 1924, the Truman's only child, Margaret, was born in an upstairs bedroom.

In 1919, Truman opened Truman & Jacobson Haberdashers in Kansas City with Army friend Eddie Jacobson. Two years later, the business failed. Truman, however, refused to declare bankruptcy and spent about the next 15 years paying off all his debts.

Truman (left, front) and his former canteen sergeant Eddie Jacobson, pose at Truman & Jacobson Haberdashers in 1919.

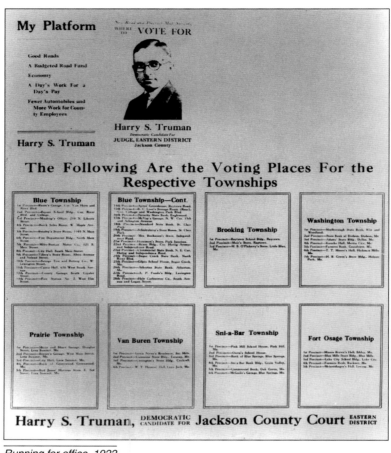

Running for office, 1922

PROUD TO BE A POLITICIAN

"I'm proud to be called politician, for it's a great honor; when a good politician dies he becomes a statesman, and I want to be a politician for a long time."

Harry S. Truman

In 1922, following the collapse of Truman & Jacobson, Truman's Army pal Jim Pendergast, nephew of Jackson County, Missouri political boss Tom Pendergast, convinced Truman to run for county judge—a position similar to county commissioner. Truman accepted and was elected with a 500 vote plurality.

Truman served as eastern judge from 1923–25, but failed to be re-elected. After a two year hiatus, Truman ran for presiding judge of the three man County Court and served in that capacity for two four-year terms.

In 1934, Truman became the Pendergast candidate for the U.S. Senate. He won the state-wide primary with 40,000 votes and in

November, easily won the Senate seat. Although known for his honesty and integrity, Truman was burdened by his association with "Boss Tom."

In the Senate, Truman was considered a "workhorse—not a showhorse." When he ran for re-election in 1940, Truman's primary victory and subsequent election came as a surprise because by this time, the Pendergast empire had been disgraced, and most predicted his defeat. From this election forward, Truman emerged very much his own man. He gained national

Senatorial candidate Harry S. Truman confidently votes for himself in the Democratic primary election, August 7, 1934.

19

An ebullient Senator Truman at the 1944 Democratic Convention.

The Truman family paused in front of a poster of President Franklin Roosevelt during the hectic 1940 re-election campaign for the United States Senate.

Vice President Harry S. Truman is seen riding with President Roosevelt in a rare photograph of the two men together.

prominence as head of the Truman Committee that investigated corruption and waste in the war effort. The success of this committee made him a prime vice-presidential running mate with Franklin Delano Roosevelt in 1944 replacing Henry Wallace.

As expected, the Roosevelt-Truman ticket won. But only 83 days after being inaugurated, Truman became the nation's 33rd president upon the death of President Roosevelt.

The following day, while talking to the press he remarked: "Boys, if you ever pray, pray for me now. I don't know whether you fellows ever had a load of hay fall on you, but when they told me yesterday what had happened, I felt like the moon, the stars, and all the planets had fallen on me."

21

Within a few hours of President Roosevelt's death, 7:09 p.m., April 12, 1945, Vice President Harry S. Truman was sworn in as President of the United States as his wife, Bess, and daughter, Margaret, looked on.

"Give 'em hell, Harry. We'll take 'em!" In one of the biggest upsets in political history, a victorious President Truman held the Chicago Daily Tribune *announcing his defeat. Few people besides Truman thought he would win, but his warmth, humor, fighting spirit and straight-talking-no-nonsense style carried the day.*

On November 7, 1948, Key West welcomed a smiling President Truman — just five days after his stunning victory over Thomas E. Dewey.

<u>VICTORY</u>

It was no easy job to follow a charismatic president like Franklin Roosevelt, who had been elected to an unprecedented four terms. As president, Harry Truman was not always popular, but his stature continues to grow with the passing years. Today, most historians classify him in the top ten of great American presidents and some place him as one of the top five. Harry Truman was never concerned with labels. He once remarked that all he knew was that he had a great time trying to be great.

MAJOR
ACCOMPLISHMENTS
AS PRESIDENT

- Authorized use of first atomic bomb against Japan which ended World War II.

- Contained the spread of Communism through collective security alliances and extensive economic aid — "Truman Doctrine," "Marshall Plan" and "Point Four."

- Launched airlift that broke the Soviet Union's blockade of West Berlin.

- Militarily resisted North Korea's invasion of South Korea.

- Fired General Douglas MacArthur when he did not follow orders.

- Stood against Senator Joseph R. McCarthy and his "red-scare" tactics.

- Initiated his "Fair Deal" program of social and economic reforms at home.

- Was a strong advocate of civil rights, outlawing segregation in the armed forces.

- Though sympathetic to labor, boldly intervened in the railroad and coal strikes of 1946 and the steel strike of 1952.

- Signed the United Nations Charter.

- Brought about North Atlantic Treaty Organization.

175 DAYS IN KEY WEST

"Wish you and Margie were here. They have fixed you up a palatial bedroom next to mine... The place is all redecorated, the porches have been leveled up so there are no steps from the dining room, new furniture and everything. I've a notion to move the capitol to Key West and just stay. Lots of Love, Harry"

Letter to Bess
March 13, 1949

President Truman played tourist in front of the Little White House in December 1947. At this time, the house was still grey and the south porch had not been extended.

After 19 months in office, President Harry S. Truman was beginning to show the effects of the unrelenting demands of the presidency. His personal physician, Brigadier General Wallace H. Graham, worried about the president's health. He had a bad cold that seemed to hang on too long. When he developed an annoying cough, the doctor ordered a vacation.

Fleet Admiral Chester W. Nimitz, Chief of Naval Operations, suggested Key West as a perfect vacation getaway. Nimitz had recently visited the Key West submarine base and had noticed the spacious, secure grounds and the large vacant commandant's home.

President Truman was very pleased when he arrived in March 1949 and discovered the newly decorated living room.

"After some investigation," Margaret Truman wrote, "Dad made a choice which he never regretted — the submarine base at Key West, Florida."

Prior to President Truman's stunning, and unexpected victory in 1948 when he was re-elected president, the Little White House remained much as it was when Captain Edwin Charles Reordan left in 1946. Following the election, however, (and perhaps because his wife and daughter accompanied him on the post-election vacation) the Navy realized the home needed to be redecorated befitting a president. The Navy hired Miami interior designer Haygood Lassiter to completely re-do the house.

The Lassiter firm had only two months and $35,000 to complete the job.

The designers made very few structural changes except for extending the south porch and adding a new flat roof (complete with sundeck) that was accessible from the second floor.

The entire house was painted, carpeted, furnished, draped and accessorized—from a pair of Staffordshire dogs to various donkey (symbol of the Democratic party) items.

Bess Truman's bedroom was the prettiest room in the refurbished Little White House.

The contract also included ordinary items like: a pad for the poker table, one jigger, lime squeezer and ice scoop, four rattan waste baskets, flower frogs, a desk blotter, leaf coasters, coat hangers and other various and sundry items from bath towels and mats to shells as planters.

Newspaper accounts remarked that the Little White House had been transformed from a fishing lodge to a home of "modest but reliable elegance."

In an article in the *Miami Herald*, Lassiter described the general scheme as "Georgetownish — gentle and restful — contemporized treatment of 18th Century Traditional and early American decor with quiet colors and lots of easy chairs and well lighted reading facilities."

Lassiter's "quiet" colors which were popular at the time included: avocado green, lime green, deep blue and chartreuse. Fabrics were bold tropical prints, plaids and stripes with colors like tomato red, olive green and lacquer red.

When the president arrived in March 1949, and saw the transformed house, he was delighted.

The north porch of the Little White House before the 1949 renovation.

The Little White House with its enlarged south porch, on the right, and new second floor sun deck.

175 DAYS
IN KEY WEST

- November 17–24, 1946

- March 12–19, 1947

- December 3–8, 1947

- February 20; February 25–March 5, 1948

- November 7–21, 1948
  (Joined by his wife, Bess, and daughter, Margaret)

- March 6–19, 1949

- November 28–December 20, 1949
  (Joined by wife, Bess, and daughter, Margaret)

- March 16–April 10, 1950
  (Bess arrived April 1)

- March 2–22, 1951

- November 8–December 9, 1951
  (Joined by wife, Bess)

- March 7–27, 1952

THE REGULARS

Chief of Staff:
  Fleet Admiral William D. Leahy
The Special Assistant to the President:
  Dr. John R. Steelman
Secretary to the President:
  William D. Hassett
Special Counsel to the President:
  Clark M. Clifford
  Charles S. Murphy
Chief of Protocol:
  Stanley Woodward
Military Aide to the President:
  Major General Harry H. Vaughan
Personal Physician to the President:
  Major General Wallace H. Graham
President's Naval Aide:
  Rear Admiral James H. Foskett
  Rear Admiral Robert L. Dennison
Air Aide to the President:
  Major General Robert B. Landry
Presidential Press Secretary:
  Charles G. Ross
Assistant Press Secretary:
  Eben A. Ayers
Administrative Assistant to the President:
  Donald S. Dawson

GOVERNMENT IN THE SUNSHINE

"Never a day goes by that I do not have to make some decision which affects the whole of the United States and sometimes the rest of the world."

Letter from Key West
November 29, 1951

WORKING VACATIONS

President Truman wrote that he used Key West more as a hideaway than a holiday. His press secretary, Charlie Ross commented that the president could get more real work done in Key West than in Washington because he could work without interruption.

In fact, some staff members recalled that they had to work harder in Key West than in Washington.

"We had to work like hell and still not give the appearance of working," reported Captain (later Admiral) Robert L. Dennison, "so it was really hell for all of us but we had our reward in knowing that he was really having a great time."

Most of the President's key staff came to Key West with him. Those closest to him stayed with him in the Little White House. Several even returned as guests after they resigned from their official duties.

The Presidential Staff at Key West in 1949: (L to R front row) Dr. John R. Steelman, Chief Justice Fred M. Vinson, President Truman, Admiral William D. Leahy, William D. Hassett, (L to R back row) William J. Bray, General Robert B. Landry, Admiral Robert L. Dennison, Stanley Woodward, Charles G. Ross, General Harry H. Vaughan, Eben A. Ayers.

31

Bess Truman would see the president off at the Washington airport.

In the early years, the president flew on the *Sacred Cow* (C-54). Later the President's plane was the *Independence* (DC-6).

The Presidential Party would arrive at the Boca Chica Naval Air Station outside Key West after a three hour, 40 minute flight.

They were greeted at the airport by Navy officers and rode in an open car motorcade from Boca Chica to the Little White House via Division Street (re-named Truman Avenue in November 1948).

When the president arrived at the Presidential Gate at the submarine base, 450 officers and enlisted personnel in white uniforms "manned the rails."

The president's flag was hoisted above the Administration Building. Usually, (except Sunday) he received full military honors, including a 21-gun salute.

As soon as Truman entered the Little White House, he telephoned his wife and changed into his casual vacation clothes.

When the Independence *arrived at Boca Chica Naval Air station, President Truman bolted down the stairs and into the warm sunshine.*

President Harry S. Truman, his wife, Bess
and daughter, Margaret, in Key West for
a visit to the Little White House in
November 1951.

POST CARD

Photograph courtesy of the Harry S. Truman Library.

President Harry S Truman in his "Key West
Uniform," accepts Florida grapefruit and
oranges from members of the Florida
Highway Patrol in front of the Little White
House in Key West, Florida.

POST CARD

Photograph courtesy of the Harry S. Truman Library.

Manning the rails

Reviewing the Marine guard

33

WHERE THEY STAYED

North bedroom—

The president

Adjoining bedroom—

Mrs. Truman and
Margaret

North center bedroom—

Admiral Foskett and
General Vaughan

South center bedroom—

Mr. Ross and
Mr. Clifford

South bedroom—

Mr. Connelly and
Dr. Steelman

2nd floor south porch—

General Graham

Bedroom on first floor—

Admiral Leahy and
Judge Collet

Overflow was housed at: the Bachelors Officer's Quarters, Quarters L and the Fleet Sonar School Bachelors Officer's Quarters. The presidential yacht, *Williamsburg,* also was used for guests.

FEEDING THE MASSES

The president and those who stayed at the Little White House ate at the dining room table. Eight Filipino cooks and stewards from the *Williamsburg* provided the meals.

The others ate at the Fleet Sonar School Officer's Mess.

The Williamsburg *docked at the north quay. It was the communication center for the Little White House and housed overflow guests. The stewards from the* Williamsburg *served the president while he was in Key West.*

Filipino stewards from the Williamsburg

General Vaughan surveyed his birthday cake, as he sat next to Margaret Truman for the evening meal.

35

THE
DAILY
SCHEDULE

- The president was an early riser and usually awoke before anyone else.

- He took a morning walk before breakfast with a member of the Secret Service.

- Ate breakfast around 7:30–8:00 a.m.

- After breakfast each morning, had an informal staff meeting and worked at his desk in the living room.

- Went to the beach at 10:00 a.m.

- Lunch at 1:00 p.m.

- Naps and reading in the afternoon.

- In the late afternoon, the president sometimes worked at the desk in his bedroom or played poker on the south porch.

- Dinner at 7:00 p.m.

- Movies after dinner each night—president usually did not attend.

- Poker on the south porch until 11:30 p.m.

KEEPING IN TOUCH

Because of Key West's isolated location, special arrangements had to be made to keep the president in touch with Washington.

TELEPHONE

The Little White House switchboard (with three direct circuits to the Washington White House) was located in Building 97 and had two operators in attendance at all times. (During one typical visit, traffic totaled 10,366 minutes.) The president usually spoke from a special phone booth in the foyer of the Little White House. A telephone was also installed in the dressing room at Truman Beach.

TELETYPE

The Navy provided teletype equipment with direct land wire service between the White House and the communications office at the submarine base. As a back-up, in case wires failed, the navy also had a radio key circuit and a radio teletype.

Classified traffic came via the *Williamsburg*-Navy Department-White House-duplex radio teletype circuit. (The commander of the naval station also set up a back-up duplex for emergency use.)

The Little White House telephone operators at work. They were the only women on the Key West staff.

Commander William M. Rigdon (right) one of President Truman's Naval aides, hands the contents of the daily mail pouch to his chief, seated at the desk in the Little White House living room. Chief Yeoman B.L. Winkler (left) takes dictation.

WRITTEN COMMUNICATION

Couriers brought the mail each day and special air mail was sent out twice a week.

Navy planes brought the official pouches from Washington three times a week. They contained executive orders for the president's signature, various memoranda from government agencies, communication from foreign governments, top secret intelligence reports, books, newspapers, weather bureau maps, reports and letters. (The president always read Mrs. Truman's letters first.)

Another set of pouches arrives in Key West with classified information for the president.

BUSINESS AS USUAL

"I have been resting very well, but the work comes along just the same."

Letter to Bess from Key West
February 28, 1948

Working on the lawn at lunch time.

STAFF

The president usually met with his staff each morning to go over the mail and sign necessary documents at his living room desk.

Occasionally he also worked in the afternoon and often took work back to his bedroom and worked at his desk there. Sometimes the president and the staff had working lunches on the Little White House lawn. Experts, cabinet members, military advisors and political leaders flew into Key West to meet with the president. Because President Truman was frequently in Key West in November, work was always done on the budget and the State of the Union Message. He flew in experts as needed.

TRANSPORTATION

The *Independence,* the president's DC-6, remained at the Boca Chica Naval Air Station in case the president needed it to return to Washington.

The *Williamsburg,* the presidential yacht, was also available as well as numerous escort boats.

AUTOMOBILES

Automobile dealers and friends in Key West and Miami loaned cars for the president's use. Sometimes, the Secret Service drove two White House cars (Lincoln convertibles) down to Key West.

SECURITY

By today's standards, security at the Little White House was minimal. Marine guards patrolled the perimeter of the house and grounds and the beach. Anyone who wanted to enter had to have a special pass signed by both the Navy and the Secret Service.

Secret Service agents, who were ultimately responsible for the president, stayed in Building 217, the Sonar School's Bachelors Officer's Quarters.

PROBLEMS, PROBLEMS

The president conferred with former Speaker of the House, Sam Rayburn, in Key West.

TRUMAN DOCTRINE

The president planned his second trip to Key West on March 8, 1947, but had to postpone it because the British had withdrawn aid to Greece and the Communists were threatening to take over.

On March 12, the president addressed a joint session of Congress, asking for $400 million in aid to Greece and Turkey. This was the greatest problem and boldest response the president had made since the war. Immediately following the speech, he left for Key West.

Soon after he arrived in Key West, he wrote to his daughter: "No one, not even me, (your mother would say), knew how worn to a frazzle the chief executive had become. The terrible decision I had to make had been over my head for about six weeks."

LABOR ISSUES

There was a great deal of labor unrest in post-war America. Although Truman thought of himself as a friend of labor, few presidents have taken as strong a stand against strikes as he did.

Margaret Truman Daniels, President Truman's daughter, wrote that "refreshed by five days of sun and thoroughly imbued with determination after his first trip to Key West, he flew home to deal with John L. Lewis, leader of the coal miners." A few days later, John L. Lewis ordered his coal miners back to work. The president also had to deal with Lewis during his November 1949 visit to Key West.

During his March 1950 visit, Truman signed an order heading off the western railroad strike. In 1952, Defense Mobilization Director Charles Wilson came to Key West to discuss the steel strike with the president.

The president and the representatives of the Joint Chiefs of Staff discussed Korean War strategy at the Key West meeting on November 28, 1951. Left to right — Mr. Matthews, General Hall and Colonel Beishline.

KOREAN WAR

In March 1951, during President Truman's first visit to Key West after the outbreak of the Korean War, he was continuing to have severe disagreement with General Douglas MacArthur over the conduct of the war and was considering MacArthur's removal from command. On April 11, 18 days after returning from Key West, Truman fired MacArthur. In response to criticism of this bold act, President Truman said his only regret was that he did not do it sooner. He later recalled, "the only thing I learned out of the whole MacArthur deal is when you feel there is something you have to do and you know in your gut you have to do it, the sooner you get it over with, the better off everybody is."

The following November, President Truman returned to Key West once more. During this visit, an unofficial cease-fire took place in Korea. On November 29, the president called in representatives of the Joint Chiefs of Staff to discuss the war and dispel rumors that peace was at hand.

About a week later, after conversations with General Omar Bradley, Chairman of the Joint Chiefs of Staff, Truman left earlier than planned and returned to Washington.

41

The president dedicates Everglades National Park.

EVERGLADES NATIONAL PARK

On Saturday, December 6, 1947, the president flew from Key West to Naples and then motored 35 miles to dedicate the new national park. He was honored at a luncheon at the Everglades Rod and Gun Club and then he drove the car back to Naples himself.

CIVIL RIGHTS

Four weeks before the president came to Key West in February–March 1948, he made a major civil rights speech which set off a revolt within the Southern wing of the Democratic Party that ultimately created the "Dixiecrat" movement.

SENATOR JOSEPH MCCARTHY

During the president's March 1950 visit to Key West, Senator Joseph McCarthy, claiming that the State Department was full of Communists, sent the president a telegram requesting limited access to the loyalty files of the State Department and blasting him for his "arrogant refusal" to open the files.

The telegram did not sway Truman and he denied McCarthy's request.

THE ELECTION OF 1952

During Truman's March 1951 visit to Key West, there was much speculation over whether he would run for re-election in 1952. During this visit, he learned that he had come in second behind Senator Estes Kefauver in the New Hampshire primary. Two days after he returned from Key West, he announced that he would not run for re-election.

OTHER NOTABLE EVENTS

During the president's December 1949 visit, the Nationalists abandoned mainland China and Chiang Kai-shek flew to Formosa.

During the president's March 1952 visit, Fulgencio Batista took over Cuba in a coup d'etat.

DATE WITH THE PRESS

"Had a press conference and it turned out well, believe it or not. The setting for it was beautiful and the press boys showed their appreciation."

Letter to Bess
February 28, 1948

"The Just One More Club," Truman's nickname for the press photographers, pose with their favorite subject on the Little White House lawn during his April 1950 visit.

President Truman had an unusually warm relationship with the press which referred to him as "Truman the Human." He enjoyed playing jokes on the press and they often played jokes on him.

Between 40 and 50 men and an occasional woman made up the presidential press corps. This included: photographers ("The Just One More Club"), correspondents, movie newsmen and in later years, a television crew.

Members of the press, like everyone else, adopted the "Key West Uniform" — a colorful tropical shirt.

Originally, most of the press stayed in the Bachelor Officer's Quarters. In later years, they stayed in town, especially at the La Concha Hotel.

The president's press secretary held a press conference each day in the lounge of the Bachelor Officer's Quarters. It was carried on the same way as in Washington.

43

The president meets the press at a March 1950 press conference on the Little White House lawn.

Presidential press conferences were usually held on the Little White House lawn with the press sitting on the grass in a circle around him. The press conferences were held in the morning — just before swimming and lasted about 20–30 minutes.

Members of the press worked at the press headquarters in the Bachelor Officer's Quarters.

FUN WITH THE PRESS

"Where have you been?" Federal Register *reporter Truman asked the startled press as they arrived in Key West on March 6, 1949.*

It was customary for the press plane to arrive before the president's plane, but on his March 1949 visit, the president's plane arrived ahead of schedule.

When the press corps disembarked, President Truman was waiting with a gold pencil and the back of an envelope poised to take notes. "Where have you been?" he queried, and then proceeded to ask the press questions.

45

"Reporter Harry" grilled the press during his December 1949 visit, while Press Secretary Charlie Ross (left) looked on with amusement.

Another time the president showed up at Press Secretary Charlie Ross' press conference at the Bachelor Officer's Quarters again saying he was a correspondent for the *Federal Register*. He then proceeded to fire off questions:

"When did you go to bed?"

"How many of you have had breakfast this morning?"

"How many of you have written your wife at least once a week since you have been down here?"

Sometimes the president invited the entire press corps to go swimming with him at Truman Beach and at least once each trip, the entire press corps was invited to lunch on the Little White House lawn.

The *Big Wheel* was always available to take members of the press fishing.

FUN IN THE SUN

"The best time I ever had was spent here in Key West while I was president."

Harry S. Truman in Key West
February 23, 1957

At "Truman Beach"

Even with the burdens of the presidency, President Truman had an uncanny ability to relax and enjoy himself—especially when he was in Key West.

His Key West "working vacations" were basically stag-parties. Some of the men, including the president, often went days without shaving.

Margaret Truman Daniels wrote that her mother stayed away because she "saw it as an all male set-up and thought Dad would have a better time horsing around with Charlie Ross and Admiral Leahy, playing poker and drinking a little bourbon beyond the range of her critical eye."

SUN AND SURF

Rarely a morning went by when the president did not spend at least two hours at "Truman Beach," located just a short distance from the Little White House. The president was not a strong swimmer but enjoyed what he called his "Missouri dog paddle" which was a sort-of side-stroke.

When the president went swimming, Navy boats kept other boaters away while lookouts watched for barracudas and other sea creatures that might endanger the president. Members of the Secret Service always swam with

47

him. Sometimes the president even swam when it was cold—forcing the shivering (and grumbling) Secret Service agents to do the same.

The president always wore his glasses while swimming. One time a large wave washed them away and even repeated dives by the Secret Service failed to retrieve them from the deep. A short while later, however, an observant Truman spied his glasses washed up on the beach. He quickly scooped them up, put them back on, and flashed the Secret Service agents one of his famous grins.

On the beach

The president also enjoyed sunning and occasionally got too much sun. "My face and head are red as a beet," he wrote his wife, "but the rest of me is brown except for a strip around the middle which is white."

He also enjoyed watching the lively volleyball games that went on almost daily.

Margaret Truman enjoyed a game of volleyball on Truman Beach with members of the president's staff.

LISTENING

The president enjoyed listening to the radio and playing the phonograph. (There was no television in Key West.) He particularly liked sports broadcasts and of course, world news and political commentary.

On his second trip, he heard his daughter, Margaret, make her radio debut. President Truman frequently spent the evening playing classical records (especially Chopin) on the phonograph. He often brought his private record collection with him to Key West.

NOW SHOWING

First run movies were shown in the living room of the Little White House every evening but the president rarely attended unless Bess and Margaret were there. He always watched the weekly newsreels, however, that were sent to Key West. After his 1948 election victory, the elated president and his party watched the newsreel account again and again.

The president and his party were off for a day of fishing aboard the crash boat Big Wheel *during his March 1949 visit.*

GONE FISHING

The "crash boat" *Dolphin* which was re-christened the *Big Wheel* was moored at the north quay and always available to take the presidential party and the press out for a day of fishing. The president was not much of a fisherman. His wife, however, loved to fish and could take any kind of rolling sea. Although he would occasionally go fishing with his staff for the camaraderie, he always went fishing with Bess when she was in town. It was customary for the fishing party to bet on the first fish, most fish, biggest fish, etc. And sometimes trophies were given to the winners.

49

The president landed a six-pound grouper off the stern of the Dolphin during his trip to the Dry Tortugas in November 1946.

Brigadier General Robert Landry, Air Force aide to the president, showed off his catch.

President Truman with Virginia Kelly the Southern International Fishing Queen, won the trophy for the Key West fishing tournament.

(Left) The president showed off a day's catch.

"Good Morning. How ya doing today?"

THE MORNING CONSTITUTION

The president began every day with a brisk walk around the naval base and sometimes into the streets of Key West. Once he stopped for a cup of coffee at the Caribe Restaurant and left an autographed dollar bill for payment. Another time he popped into the Key West Aquarium and asked the startled owner for a tour.

He also loved to surprise the sailors as he walked around the base. One time he walked in on a group of men in the shower and another time went into the barracks before reveille and woke them up! He also liked to drop into the enlisted men's mess and line up for a meal.

THE ROUTE

When he walked about town he usually left by the Green Street gate and would proceed east along Green Street to Simonton, south on Simonton to Southard, west on Southard and back to the naval station.

51

The president startled everyone when he took the wheel and drove away from the Little White House.

HARRY AT THE WHEEL

It seems hard to believe today, in an era of tight security, that President Truman often drove himself around in an open convertible. Once he drove 40 miles up the Overseas Highway and wrote his wife that he "almost scared the men at the first toll gate to death when we drove up." When he went to dedicate the Everglades National Park, he did the driving on the return trip between Naples and the park.

SIDE TRIPS

Sometimes the president and his family left Key West for brief trips to other places. One of his favorite side trips was to Fort Jefferson on Dry Tortugas. Once Margaret and Bess went to Havana to shop and had tea with President Carlos Prio's wife and family.

The presidential party visited Fort Jefferson at Dry Tortugas.

THE KEY WEST UNIFORM

Following the 1948 election, Miami publicist Hank Meyer came up with the idea of sending the president four colorful sport shirts from one of his clients — Miamian Ben Bloom of Royal Palm Sportswear. Truman loved the shirts and not only wore them himself, he also encouraged members of his staff to wear them as well. Pictures of the president in "that shirt" made front page stories across the nation.

The subsequent publicity started a craze which continued for the rest of his visits to Key West. So many people began sending him shirts that he would spread a dozen or so out and let people take their pick of what quickly became known as the "Key West Uniform."

"TAKE YOUR PICK BOYS!"
Everyone wore one of the colorful shirts sent to the president while he was in Key West.

53

President Truman, dressed in the original "Key West Uniform" sent to him by Miami publicist Hank Meyer, accepted some Florida grapefruit from members of the Florida Highway Patrol.

Margaret Truman wore her "Key West Uniform" while walking with her father and members of his party.

"VISITING WITH MEMBERS OF HIS PARTY"

President Truman loved to play poker but since it involved gambling, it was not something that was publicized. In fact, it was covered up. In the detailed logs of his visits to Key West, the cryptic "where he visited with members of his party" referred to the nightly poker game on the south porch of the Little White House.

The poker table at which the president "visited with members of his party."

ROUNDING UP A QUORUM

After dinner, the president would announce to vacation coordinator Navy Lt. Commander William M. Rigdon, "Bill, round up a quorum."

The men would gather around the special poker table that the Navy built and "visit" until about 11:30 p.m.

Participants reported that it was a wild game.

The president was described as an excellent (but too optimistic) player. Because he really didn't want to win and take money away from his staff, he always stayed until the last card.

Each trip the players would put $50–$75 into the pot. Bets were limited to $2. When a player lost his initial stake, the banker (who was usually Gen. Vaughan) would "put him on poverty" and give him $10. If that was lost too, another $10 was forthcoming. Thus, no one could lose more than their initial $50–$75 during the whole vacation. Usually, no one, except the president, ever won or lost more than $30.

President Truman and members of his party were known to "horse around" during the nightly "quorum" on the south porch.

President Truman and his grandsons take a stroll during his 1968 visit to Key West.

KEY WEST AT SUNSET

"Never have we had such a wonderful vacation as we did on our trip to Key West.... We are anxious to get back for more Key West sunshine."

Letter from Bess Truman to
Mary and John Spottswood
May 7, 1968

SAND IN HIS SHOES

Harry S. Truman never got the Key West sand out of his shoes. On March 27, 1952, when he left Key West for the last time as president, he promised to return. He kept his word.

Beginning in 1957, and continuing until 1969, "Citizen" Truman, as he liked to call himself, came to Key West five more times.

During each of these visits he and his wife, (and sometimes his daughter, son-in-law and his grandchildren), stayed with his closest Key West friends, John and Mary Spottswood.

The Trumans' friendship with the Spottswoods was sparked when John Spottswood, owner of radio station WKWF—a Mutual Broadcast station—arranged to switch to ABC for one hour so he could broadcast Margaret Truman's radio debut.

Except for his last visit in 1969, when he was recovering from the flu, the former president took his famous walks around the streets of Key West and visited the Little White House. Sometimes he held a press conference.

On April 5, 1969, when Truman and his wife flew out of Key West for the last time, the Spottswoods discovered that the former president had absent-mindedly left his favorite old brown hat on the seat of their Cadillac limousine. Perhaps, he hoped that one day he would be back to get it.

Presidential friend John Spottswood had a special license tag made for the car the president used while he was in Key West.

The presidential gate at the Truman Annex.

An aging former president bids farewell to Key West.

"KEY WEST LOSES A FRIEND"

Harry S. Truman, died on December 26, 1972.

Two days later, the citizens of Key West gathered
on "Truman Beach" for a memorial service.
As taps was played,
Key West Mayor John H. McCoy,
along with
Rear Admiral John H. Maurer, commander of the naval base,
placed a wreath into the waters.

Two years later, the former naval station was re-named the
Naval Air Station
Harry S. Truman Annex.

December 28, 1972, Key West Mayor John H. McCoy and Rear Admiral John H. Maurer, commander of the Key West Naval Base, placed a wreath into the waters off "Truman Beach" as part of a memorial service honoring President Harry S. Truman.

Alfred Colebook rendered "Taps" from "Truman Beach" as part of the memorial services.

ACKNOWLEDGMENTS

More than anything else, this book is a guide book to the Harry S. Truman Little White House in Key West, Florida and grew out of research for that project. Its purpose is to give visitors more information about the very human side of President Truman, which was so evident during his 175 happy and productive days in Key West.

I am grateful to Pritam Singh, who hired me in 1989 to do the research and interpretation for the Little White House Museum, to Bud and Mary Drettmann, who completed the museum and opened it to the public in April 1991, and to Elizabeth K. Ehrbar, who has been my partner in the entire project.

Others who have been extremely helpful include: staff of the Truman Library in Independence, Missouri: Dr. Benedict Zobrist, director, Pauline Testerman, Erwin J. Mueller, Clay Bauske, Millie Carol, Pat Dorsey and Mark Beverage; Liz Newland, director of the Little White House Museum; Sharon Wells of the Historic Key West Preservation Board and Tom Hambrick of the Monroe County Library.

As usual, editor and friend, Howard Kleinberg, has been invaluable along with my assistants Cheryl Frary, Regina Dodd and April Bolet. Special thanks also goes to David McCullough and members of the Reordan family.

All photographs are courtesy of the Truman Library in Independence, Missouri, except for: page 4, William Reordan; 7, 8 (top), National Archives; 8 (bottom) Katy Truitt; 9, Monroe County Public Library; 17, 18, *Kansas City Star* (Mercantile Library Association); 20 (bottom), *St. Louis Globe Democrat*; 21, 26, 38, 48 (bottom), 49, 52 (top), *The Miami News*.

BIBLIOGRAPHY
AND NOTES

Ferrell, Robert H. *Dear Bess*. New York: W.W. Norton & Co., 1983.

Ferrell, Robert H. *A Centenary Remembrance*. New York: Viking Press, 1984.

Goldman, Eric F. *The Crucial Decade—And After*. New York: Vintage Books, 1960.

Miller, Merle. *Plain Speaking: An Oral Biography of Harry S. Truman*. New York: Berkley Medallion Books, 1973.

Rigdon, William M. *White House Sailor*. New York: William Morrow & Co., Inc., 1973.

Truman, Margaret. *Bess W. Truman*. New York: MacMillan Publishing Co., 1987.

————————. *Harry S. Truman*. New York: William Morrow & Co., 1973.

————————. *Where the Buck Stops* . New York: Warner Books, Inc., 1989.

Truman, Harry S. *Memoirs of Harry S. Truman, 1945-52*. New York: Da Capo Press, Inc., 1956.

The Truman Years. Waukesha, Wisconsin: Country Beautiful, 1976.

TRUMAN LIBRARY: MANUSCRIPTS, ETC.

Family Correspondence: 1945–1959

Oral Histories: Eben Ayers, Clark Clifford, Carlton Kent, Robert Dennison, Milton Kayle, Charles S. Murphy.

Presidential Secretary's File: Key West

Rigdon, William M., ed. *Log of the President's Vacation Trip to Key West, Florida*. *1st Trip: November 17–23, 1946; 3rd Trip: December 3–8, 4th Trip: February 20–March 5, 5th Trip: November 7–21, 1948; 6th Trip: March 6–19, 1949, 7th Trip: November 28–December 20, 1949; 8th Trip: March 12–April 10, 1950; 10th Trip: November 8–December 9, 1951; 11th Trip: March 7–17, 1952.*

Truman: Key West, Florida: Vertical File

OTHER

Presidential Clipping Files, Monroe County Library

The Miami News, Dates of all Presidential Trips

NOTES ON THE TEXT

8 "we had...almost anything." Margaret Truman, *Bess W. Truman* (New York: MacMillan, 1987), p. 388.

26 "after some investigation...Key West, Florida." Margaret Truman, *Harry S. Truman* (New York: Morrow, 1973), p. 323.

40 "refreshed...coal miners." *Ibid.*, p.324.

41 "the only thing...everybody is." Merle Miller, *Plain Speaking* (New York: Berkley, 1973), p. 313.

47 "saw it ...critical eye." Margaret Truman, *Bess W. Truman*, p. 350.

In November 1952, President Truman enjoyed the beach during his last presidential visit to Key West.